JESUS >
RELIGION
STUDENT BIBLE STUDY

LifeWay Press®
Nashville, Tennessee

Published by LifeWay Press® • © 2014 Jefferson Bethke

ISBN: 9781430039716
Item number: P005720368

Dewey Decimal Classification Number: 248.83
Subject Heading: JESUS CHRIST \ CHRISTIAN LIFE \ GRACE (THEOLOGY)

Printed in the United States of America

Student Ministry Publishing
LifeWay Church Resources
One LifeWay Plaza
Nashville, TN 37234-0144

We believe that the Bible has God for its author; salvation for its end;
and truth, without any mixture of error, for its matter
and that all Scripture is totally true and trustworthy.
To review LifeWay's doctrinal guideline,
please visit *www.lifeway.com/doctrinalguideline*.

contents

ABOUT THE AUTHOR 4

SESSION 1: JESUS > RELIGION 5

SESSION 2: LOVE > SELF 17

SESSION 3: GIVER > GIFTS 29

SESSION 4: COVENANT > CONTRACT 41

SESSION 5: WORSHIP > RITUALS 53

SESSION 6: COMMUNITY > CONFORMITY 65

POEM: WHY I HATE RELIGION BUT LOVE JESUS 78

ABOUT JEFFERSON BETHKE

HEY, GUYS! The first time meeting someone is always awkward, so I thought I'd start by sharing a little bit about myself.

I was born in Tacoma, Washington.
I played baseball in college.
I graduated with a degree in politics and government.
I co-own a company called Claro Candles, which donates its profits
 to combat injustice around the world.
I have a dog named Aslan (for Narnia!).
I'm married to an amazing, beautiful, sweet woman of God: Alyssa.
I'm a dad! Kinsley Joy Bethke is my sweet little daughter.
I wrote a book (so surreal!).
I like to make creative videos.

Enough about me. I'd love to hear about you and your story as it pertains to our Bible study together. Feel free to share, critique, question, or just say hello. My contact information is below. And use **#JesusIsGreater** to share any thoughts with the world.

TWITTER *www.twitter.com/jeffersonbethke*
INSTAGRAM*www.instagram.com/jeffersonbethke*
PINTEREST *www.pinterest.com/jeffersonbethke*

FACEBOOK *www.facebook.com/jeffersonbethkepage*
YOUTUBE *www.youtube.com/bball1989*
BLOG *www.jeffbethke.com*

For more on this subject, consider reading *Jesus > Religion: Why He is so Much Better than Trying Harder, Doing More, and Being Good Enough* by Jefferson Bethke (Nelson Books, 2013, ISBN 978-1-4002-0539-4).

session one
JESUS>RELIGION

"The Jesus of the Bible is a radical man with a radical message, changing people's lives in a radical way."

start

Each of us walk into certain situations with expectations. Those expectations could be high or low and are usually based on previous experiences or preconceived notions.

When have you been surprised by something that turned out better than you expected?

Reflect on a time when you missed out on something great or found yourself in an awkward situation because of a misunderstanding?

Over the next six weeks you will be challenged to set aside your preconceived ideas about religion and honestly consider (or reconsider) the person of Jesus. The question to keep in mind as we begin our study and watch the first video is this:

WHAT IF LIFE WITH JESUS IS BETTER THAN YOU THOUGHT?

watch
HIGHLIGHTS FROM "JESUS > RELIGION" VIDEO.

REMEMBER THIS 🔊

> Christianity is not about us coming to God. It's about God coming to us.
> Rules and institutions are beautiful when they are a response to a relationship.
> We all struggle. We're all frail, broken, messed-up people.
> We're all looking to be known, to be loved, to have purpose. Only Jesus can provide that.

THINK ABOUT THIS ❓

> How would your life be different if you really understood that Jesus is the only One who can give you joy, hope, peace, and life?

LOOK IT UP 📖

> Hebrews 3:1, 4:14, 7:27
> 1 Corinthians 3:16
> Revelation 21:22
> Psalm 32:9
> Isaiah 30:16
> John 1:14
> 1 Peter 2:24
> Ephesians 2:1
> Romans 3:10-12, 4:5, 7:18-19

consider

What does being a Christian mean to you? Explain.

Let's look to the ultimate source for understanding Christianity and make sure our view lines up with the Bible.

Read Ephesians 2:4-10.

What aspects of God's character stand out in these verses?

What do these verses say about Jesus?

Read Romans 8:10-11.

According to this passage, what is our hope based on?

What earthly things have you placed your hope and happiness in? What is the danger of putting your hope in anyone or anything besides Jesus?

Read Romans 4:4-5.

How does the fact that God justifies the ungodly give you freedom in life?

Are you encouraged to hear that the Bible is full of broken, messed up people who were loved and changed by God's grace? Explain.

What else did Jeff say in the video that was encouraging, convicting, or helpful?

respond

Jeff shared that he tried religion and walked away from it, only to realize that he misunderstood Jesus and what being a Christian is really about.

Is your understanding of Christianity centered on religion or a relationship with Jesus? Explain.

JESUS> RELIGION

We talked about a lot of things in our first session together. Maybe some ideas, thoughts, or questions were stirred up inside of you. It may have even opened some old wounds, but hopefully it gave you the opportunity to open up your heart and mind, let down your guard, and to consider whether or not the Jesus you've believed in (or have chosen not to believe in) is the real Jesus.

The real Jesus can change your life.

Each week you'll have the opportunity to continue searching and reflecting on what you are learning. You'll find three personal reading segments for you to complete on your own between the group times. This aspect of the study is significant to your individual growth and personal understanding of who Jesus is. Carve out time in the days ahead to dig into God's Word using the following pages as a guide.

FOR MORE, READ CHAPTERS 1-3 IN THE BOOK: *JESUS > RELIGION*.

MORE THAN A RULE BOOK
read

The Bible isn't filled with squeaky-clean, picture-perfect stories. The great heroes of the faith aren't all that heroic, actually. They're pretty normal. Sometimes, it is even shocking to read about some of their failures, rebellion, doubts, and struggles. But that's also what is so significant and encouraging about the Bible. It's a grand narrative of God's grace. It's a love story and an epic battle. Jesus is the hero. Not us. It's a great rescue mission and restoration project. God is fixing everything we've broken throughout history.

If you just think of the Bible as an old book full of rules, a checklist of do's and don'ts, or a collection of inspirational stories, you're missing out. The Bible is so much greater than that.

How would you describe the Bible to someone? Why is it different from all other books?

How significant is the Bible to your everyday life? How often do you read it?

Because we're going to be reading the Bible throughout this study, let's do two things. First, let's see what the Bible says about itself. Then, we'll look at an example of a real person in Scripture, as he expressed real feelings, to a real God.

Begin by reading what Jesus says about Scripture:

"You search the Scriptures because you think that in them you have eternal life; and it is they that bear witness about me, yet you refuse to come to me that you may have life." John 5:39-40

Basically, Jesus was saying that there are two ways of viewing Scripture. We can either look at it, or we can look through it. The Bible can either be a wall or a windshield. Jesus told the religious teachers of His day that it was not enough to know what the Scriptures said if they didn't have a relationship with the God who said it. The Bible isn't a moral checklist to read, highlight, and memorize your way into a better life (now and eternally). The Bible is intended to help us see Jesus clearly as we follow Him wherever He leads us.

Circle the way you view Scripture: wall or windshield

Now, let's look at a psalm of David as he shared real feelings in a real relationship with a real God.

Read Psalm 19.

Can you relate to the writer of this psalm? What emotions are expressed?

What does this psalm teach you about a relationship with God?

What does this psalm say about the Word of God?

TAKE TIME TO KNOW GOD. TO HEAR HIS WORD. TO SEE JESUS.

reflect

Use this space to creatively reflect on the fact that God wants to speak to you through His Word. Draw, journal, or list your thoughts.

Share your thoughts: #JesusIsGreater

MORE THAN A RELIGION
read

Let's start with this pivotal question:

Are you a Christian?

Now, you may have answered that question like many of us do. "Sure, of course, I am (I mean, I'm not some other religion). I go to church (or I have gone some). I have a Bible (maybe a Bible app). I try to do the right things (most of the time). I believe in God (or something)."

Or maybe you responded "no." But there's something in you that's at least interested enough in Jesus to be reading this right now. Or maybe you're just at the end of your rope. Everything seems to be unraveling, so why not give religion a try? Maybe you're doing this just because someone asked you to.

Whatever your reason or what you think your reason is, take some time to consider this question:

What if God is real? What if the reason you are reading this right now is because God wants you to know Him? Do you believe you can really know God?

In the group session, we defined religion as things we do to try to get God's approval or hopefully get into heaven. Grace is the exact opposite. Religion is trying to climb the ladder up to God. Grace is God coming down to us and giving us eternal life through what Jesus has done.

We're going to talk a lot about grace throughout this study. God's Word is full of incredible stories of grace that show us why a relationship with Jesus is so much greater than religion.

Read Acts 9:1-19.

Two thousand years ago this super religious guy named Saul (his Hebrew name), later known as Paul (his Greek name), became one of the most influential people in history. He had been such a devout Jew that he hated this new group of Jews who claimed that Jesus was the Son of God. Paul began tracking down followers of Jesus and persecuting them, but God had a very different plan.

Read Acts 11:25-26.

The early Christians lived radically different from their culture. Religious and political leaders felt threatened by them because their faith was turning the world upside down (see Acts 17:6).

> I count everything as loss because of the surpassing worth of knowing Christ Jesus my Lord. For his sake I have suffered the loss of all things and count them as rubbish, in order that I may gain Christ and be found in him, not having a righteousness of my own that comes from the law, but that which comes through faith in Christ, the righteousness from God that depends on faith. Philippians 3:8-9

When it came to practicing religion, Paul had every gold star imaginable. He knew all the right answers, obeyed all the right rules, led the most elite groups, and was born into the right family. But when compared to his relationship with Jesus, all his religious accolades were worthless.

What about you? Are you trying to earn God's favor by working harder to be good? If so, why do you think that is?

CHRISTIANITY IS A RELATIONSHIP WITH JESUS BY GRACE, NOT EFFORT.

reflect

How is having a relationship with Jesus so much more than a religion?

💬 Share your thoughts: #JesusIsGreater

MORE THAN A GOOD MAN
read

There's a certain Bible verse that's almost become a cliché. We see it everywhere, but many people have no idea what it really means. It's John 3:16.

> God so loved the world, that he gave his only Son, that whoever believes in him should not perish but have eternal life. John 3:16

The story surrounding this verse is too good to miss.

Read John 3:1-21.

There's a lot going on in this story, but here are a few things we need to notice:

1 Nicodemus was a Pharisee, meaning he was a religious leader.

2 Nicodemus came at night to meet with Jesus. Most likely, Nicodemus didn't want his religious friends to see him asking Jesus questions. It's interesting to note that Jesus also used light and dark to represent being in or out of relationship with God.

3 Nicodemus didn't understand what Jesus was talking about because it didn't fit into his mindset for relating to God.

How has your understanding of Jesus changed over time? Explain.

Nicodemus called Jesus "Rabbi" and then said, "We know that you are a teacher come from God" (v. 2). But Nicodemus's words show that he didn't know who Jesus really was.

What are some popular opinions about Jesus today?

Who do you say Jesus is? Explain.

Jesus said we either believe in Him for salvation or we don't. There's no middle ground. In each pair of words or phrases, underline the one that applies to your life right now.

Light	Dark
Eternal life	Death
Believing in Jesus	Not so sure yet
Living for God	Living for this physical world

Jesus came to bring us life, but He didn't come to get rid of everything we might associate with religion. He came to put everything back in its rightful place. Things were all mixed up and out of order. Just as they are today.

Read Matthew 5:17-20.

Basically, Jesus said unless you're better at keeping all the rules than the Pharisees (like Nicodemus), then your religion will never earn your way into heaven. In other words, none of us are climbing that ladder and reaching the top. Religion says do. Jesus says done. But He didn't say that what's written in Scripture isn't true. Every bit of it is true. And it points to Jesus.

IT'S ALL ABOUT JESUS.

reflect

Use this space to express your thoughts and feelings about the person of Jesus.

Share your thoughts: #JesusIsGreater

session two
LOVE>SELF

"Jesus completely shattered the social, gender, and economic paradigms. Such barriers didn't exist to Him, and it was the same in the early church."

start

Our culture thrives on the comparison game—which athlete is more talented, which model is more beautiful, which company is more successful. It's easy to get caught up in this mindset and begin to compare ourselves to different standards, hoping we measure up in the end.

How often are you tempted to compare yourself to others? When is the last time you remember doing so?

Are you more likely to compare yourself to people you think are better than you? Or to those you feel you are better than? Why?

It is human nature to constantly make comparisons. Keep the following question in mind as you watch the next video:

DO YOU LOOK TO JESUS OR TO PEOPLE WHEN MEASURING YOUR WORTH?

watch

USE THIS SPACE TO FOLLOW ALONG AS YOU WATCH "LOVE > SELF."

REMEMBER THIS

> When you make something other than Jesus central, that's idolatry.
> Comparison is an endless cycle.
> God doesn't grade on a curve; He grades on a cross.
> God has rescued us through the person and work of Jesus.

THINK ABOUT THIS

> Do you understand that Jesus doesn't go around you, He goes straight to you?
> In light of the grace you've been given, do you point others to grace?

LOOK IT UP

> John 4:1-42
> Ephesians 6:12
> Colossians 1:21
> Romans 5:10
> 2 Corinthians 5:21
> Hebrews 4:15
> Matthew 22:36-40

consider

Let's start with the questions Jeff asked at the end of the video:

How have you experienced the cycle of disappointment that occurs when you compare yourself to others?

What do you think Jeff meant when he said, "God doesn't grade on a curve; He grades on a cross?"

How have you experienced God's grace? In what ways have you shared it with others?

Read John 4:1-30.

In Jesus' day, Jews and Samaritans were bitter rivals. Often, Jews would journey around Samaria to avoid any interaction with Samaritans.

Why do you think Jesus went through Samaria instead of going around it?

What struggles in your life or in the lives of others seem too sinful for Jesus to change?

Jeff pointed out that people often demonize the opposite of what they idolize. In other words, people are threatened by anything or anyone in competition with what they love. So much so, that they often attempt to discredit or make the other side look wicked in some way or another.

How have you seen people demonize the opposite of what they idolize?

How does grace change the endless cycle of comparison?

respond

Consider the fact that Jesus doesn't go around you, He's not afraid of your sin, and He comes to you right where you are.

How does that reality bring you hope? Explain.

LOVE>
SELF

When you learn to see yourself and others through the eyes of Jesus, your life will be radically changed. He loves you. Don't just skip over that. You. Are. Loved.

God doesn't love the person you wish you were or the person you pretend to be. He loves you. The real you.

How freeing is that?

Many of us spend our lives comparing ourselves to others, hoping we can be good enough. But seeking identity and worth in anything other than Jesus is a never-ending cycle of disappointment. Our identity and worth are found only in Him.

To wrap our hearts and minds around just how explosive and powerful this truth is, we're going to look at three ideas:

1 Grace is more than we deserve.
2 Humility means thinking of yourself less.
3 Love is the greatest commandment.

FOR MORE, READ CHAPTERS 4–5 IN THE BOOK: *JESUS > RELIGION*.

MORE THAN WE DESERVE
read

Grace is scandalous. It's more than we deserve. In fact, grace is getting something we don't deserve at all. It's a good gift we could never earn (see Romans 11:6). When we introduced grace last week, we learned that it's the opposite of religion—the opposite of trying harder to do the right things to deserve God's favor. Now, let's move beyond the concept and see how grace transforms our lives.

Read John 4:1-6.

Religion makes enemies. Jesus makes friends. He doesn't go around us. He comes straight to us. Recall in the group session we learned that Jews and Samaritans were bitter rivals. The root of this disdain and prejudice was religious. Jews viewed Samaritans as people who had compromised the purity of the Jewish religion by integrating into a foreign culture. But instead of dismissing and avoiding people, Jesus had to go to them (see verse 4). His mission on this earth was to extend God's love and grace to whoever would believe in Him (see John 3:16.)

Who do you avoid? Why?

How would you feel if God wanted to change their lives? Would you celebrate the change, or would you question God? What does your response reveal about your perspective of grace?

Read John 4:7-15.

The woman immediately questioned Jesus from a cultural and religious perspective. But Jesus wasn't deterred by her questions. He put the religious and cultural differences aside and got personal.

Read John 4:16-30.

Notice that when Jesus got personal, the woman turned the conversation into a religious debate. But Jesus is greater than religion. He kept the conversation focused on her need for love and grace. He offered her the very thing she had presumably been seeking in relationships with men. The living water Jesus offers is eternally satisfying.

What have you filled your life with in an effort to find satisfaction and relief?

Read John 4:39-42.

After experiencing the unconditional grace of Jesus, the woman ran to tell others.

Have you experienced the grace of Jesus personally or have you only heard others talk about it? Explain.

Who do you know who needs to experience the grace of Jesus for themselves?

JESUS DOESN'T AVOID YOU. HE COMES TO GIVE YOU GRACE.

reflect

Consider the fact that Jesus meets you where you are, knows everything about you, and offers grace.

What is your response to His amazing grace?

💬 Share your thoughts: #JesusIsGreater

THINKING OF YOURSELF LESS
read

Define humility in your own words.

We've already established that religion is focused on you. It's about what you need to do right. This effort to perform naturally leads to pride for getting things right or to self-loathing for getting things wrong. Both of these miss the bull's-eyes of godly humility, which is focused on Jesus.

Read Romans 12:2-3.

How can you break free from a worldly perspective?

What does verse 3 say about humility?

Read Romans 12:4-5.

When your identity and worth are found in your relationship to Jesus, you're freed from the endless cycle of comparing yourself to others. You don't have to one-up and outdo anyone. People are no longer competition when you aren't living to prove yourself to anyone else. You're living to please God.

Recall Paul's words to the Ephesians that we looked at in session one.

> For by grace you have been saved through faith. And this is not your own doing; it is the gift of God, not a result of works, so that no one may boast. EPHESIANS 2:8-9

How do these verses absolutely destroy religious effort, pride, and comparison to others?

The truth is that you're loved and accepted by God's grace alone—not by your works—so you have nothing to boast about. That doesn't mean you won't still be tempted to compare yourself to others. You may be tempted to feel you're better than people who don't know Jesus yet. Or those who know Jesus but aren't as good at doing the right things as you are. But Jesus leaves no room for pride and comparison. Everyone needs His love and grace.

Read John 8:1-11.

This is another story about the beautiful and scandalous grace of Jesus. Put yourself in this scene. One moment this woman was involved in the act of adultery, the next she was seized by religious leaders, forced into the public, and then she was lying at the feet of Jesus. Let that shock sink in. Feel the crushing weight of the religious leaders' pride and arrogance—the hateful self-righteousness that so desperately wanted to be right that it was willing to throw rocks at this woman…until she died.

What do Jesus' responses to the Pharisees and to the woman reveal about pride and humility?

DON'T THINK TOO MUCH OF YOURSELF OR TOO LITTLE OF OTHERS. WE ALL NEED GOD'S GRACE.

reflect

How are you like the woman in John 8? How are you like the Pharisees?

Share your thoughts: #JesusIsGreater

THE GREATEST COMMANDMENTS
read

Jesus was so radically different from anyone who had ever lived that people weren't sure what to do with Him. Jesus didn't fit into the religious mold of His day.

Religious leaders were constantly challenging Jesus. They wanted to prove they were right and continually tried to trap Him into saying or doing something wrong. There were two primary religious groups in Scripture who had a competitive attitude toward Jesus. Viewing Him as a threat to their status and influence among the people, they treated Jesus like an opponent to defeat and eventually as an enemy to kill (see John 11:45-53).

1 The Sadducees, the priestly class that ran the temple, were generally highly educated and wealthy. Pride kept them from what they couldn't explain or control.

2 The Pharisees were fundamentalists and legalists; they loved being better than everyone. Pride made them constantly obsess over every detail in their pursuit of perfection.

Ironically, both groups seemed to believe they had God on their side.

Read Matthew 22:34-40.

The Sadducees' attempt to outsmart Jesus and publicly embarrass Him backfired miserably, so the Pharisees called in an expert. The question the lawyer asked Jesus wasn't sincere. It was a political trap to get Jesus to take sides for or against popular schools of thought, therefore discrediting Him as a Teacher of the law. But again, this tactic backfired when Jesus provided an irrefutable summary of the entire law.

What did Jesus say are the two greatest commandments?

What do these two commands have in common?

It's not enough to do what we think proves our love for God if we don't also have a love for people. So, our natural response is then to narrowly define exactly whom we have to love.

Read Matthew 5:38-48.

The love of God is radically humble. It's bigger than you. It's meant to be shared with the people around you—people you like and people you don't.

How is humility at the heart of the kind of love Jesus described?

Religion puts up walls. It leads to an endless cycle of comparison. Jesus tears down barriers and bridges gaps, bringing people together. He removes sin and its consequences, making new life possible. Unlike the religious leaders, who were known for their traditions and morality, Jesus said His disciples would be known by their love:

"A new commandment I give to you, that you love one another: just as I have loved you, you also are to love one another. By this all people will know that you are my disciples, if you have love for one another." JOHN 13:34-35

LOVE GOD. LOVE PEOPLE. ALL OF THEM. THERE'S NOTHING GREATER.

reflect

When people look at you, do they see the love of Jesus? What changes do you need to make?

Share your thoughts: #JesusIsGreater

session three
GIVER>GIFTS

"Jesus doesn't promise us worldly success,
He promises Himself."

start

Session two focused on grace, humility, and love. In this session, we'll shift our focus to blessings and joy.

What is the greatest gift you have ever received? Why?

Is there anything in your life that you'd be devastated by if it was lost or taken? Explain.

Sometimes we value something in and of itself. Other times—and most often with gifts—the value of something is enhanced by the relationship of the person who gave it to us or the history behind it. Keep the following question in mind as you watch the next video:

DO YOU LOVE JESUS FOR WHO HE IS OR FOR WHAT YOU HOPE TO GET OUT OF THE DEAL?

watch

USE THIS SPACE TO FOLLOW ALONG AS YOU WATCH "GIVER > GIFTS."

REMEMBER THIS 🗨

> The root of sin in our lives is idolatry.
> Anything we worship other than Jesus is an idol.
> God is saying these things about idolatry because He wants to give us the most joy possible.
> When your hope and identity is in the Creator, true joy is found.

THINK ABOUT THIS ❓

> If everything in your life was taken away, would Jesus be enough for you?
> Are you following God to get His gifts or to get Him?

LOOK IT UP 📖

> Romans 1:25, 8:35-39
> James 1:17
> Exodus 20:1-17
> John 10:10, 15:11
> Matthew 6:19-21
> Hebrews 6:17-20, 12:28
> Ephesians 1:3

consider

Let's start with some questions Jeff asked in the video:

If everything in your life were taken away, would Jesus be enough?

When have you tried to use God to get things you wanted?

Read Matthew 6:19-21.

What does Jesus teach about the source of our hope and happiness?

Read Romans 8:35-39.

What encouragement do these verses provide about the love of Jesus and your circumstances?

Read James 1:17.

When do you most often focus on gifts instead of the Giver?

How can you focus on the Giver instead of just gifts? List some steps you can take to help shift your focus today.

Read John 10:10 and 15:11.

What does Jesus want to give us?

respond

How would you answer the question Jeff asked in the video: "What's the point of following Jesus?"

GIVER>
GIFTS

Jesus is more satisfying than anything in this world. Another form of comparison and self focus is to believe that if God is good and really loves you, He'll bless you with more things. Health, wealth, and success are not signs of God's favor or a right relationship with Him. To desire God's gifts more than God Himself as the Giver, is idolatry and will never satisfy us. To know and trust Jesus gives rest and joy greater than any circumstance, good or bad. God does not delight in suffering, but He does use it to bring about growth and beauty. This week we will focus on how Jesus is enough:

1 Idolatry: too much of a good thing
2 Every good & perfect gift
3 More than this world

Trusting Jesus gives us rest and joy. He not only gives good things, but He is every good gift we will ever need. Our hope and satisfaction is in God's love for us in Jesus and the promise of all things being made right (resurrection, justice, healing). Jesus is enough.

FOR MORE, READ CHAPTERS 6–7 IN THE BOOK: *JESUS > RELIGION*.

TOO MUCH OF A GOOD THING
read

Do you ever view God like Santa Claus? I don't mean imagining Him with a white beard and living far away in a magical place on top of the world. What I mean is, have you ever acted as if God exists just to give you what you want as long as you're good enough to deserve it? And Santa grades on a pretty easy curve when it comes to naughty and nice, right? So as long as we're not awful compared to other people, we should get what we want.

This is how I used to view God at times. If I was at least as good as everyone else, I expected to have a pretty good life and to get into heaven when I died. Basically, this is using God, not loving Him. It's treating God like a vending machine. You're putting something into your relationship with God only to get something out of it. It's all about you and what you want.

To put this in biblical terms, we're talking about idolatry. That might sound pretty harsh and foreign, right? After all, you probably don't worship statues made of wood, stone, or precious metals. But in Colossians, Paul explained that covetousness is idolatry.

> Put to death therefore what is earthly in you: sexual immorality, impurity, passion, evil desire, and covetousness, which is idolatry. COLOSSIANS 3:5

Covetousness is like greed and jealousy rolled into one desire. To covet is to want something that someone else has—and maybe even believe you deserve it at least as much as, if not more than, they do. Covetousness is an insatiable hunger. No matter what you get, you'll never be satisfied.

What or who have you felt that you had to have in order to be fulfilled?

Did you get what you wanted? If so, how long were you satisfied?

Read Exodus 20:3-4 and Romans 1:21-25.

What do these verses reveal about idolatry?

Worship means making something the ultimate object of your affection—a relationship, an activity, an achievement, a possession, or an experience. Whatever motivates your decisions, influences your lifestyle, consumes your thoughts, and excites your passion is an object of worship.

Who or what is most important in your life? (Consider this question honestly. Nobody else has to see your answer.)

Often idolatry takes the form of turning something good into our god. It's putting the created thing in the place of our Creator (see Rom. 1:25). Idolatry is an unhealthy and disproportionate amount of affection we've placed on anything other than God. Too much of a good thing becomes a really bad thing.

God isn't a vending machine, a genie in a bottle, or a cosmic Santa Claus to be used for what we can get from Him. He alone is worthy of our worship. He's the One who created us and the things we're tempted to love more than Him. He alone can satisfy us. He alone can truly love us in return and give us what we need, even if it isn't always what we want.

NO CREATED THING IS GREATER THAN THE ONE WHO CREATED IT.

reflect

Use this space to express your thanks and praise to God for who He is, not what He gives you.

💬 Share your thoughts: #JesusIsGreater

EVERY GOOD & PERFECT GIFT
read

A better way to view God than the Santa Claus image is as our Father. This is a common description of God in the Bible and the term Jesus used often.

What do you think of when you hear the word *father*?

Whether you have a positive, negative, or mixed reaction to that word, based on your personal experiences, you can be sure God is the perfect Father. He's what a father should be.

Read James 1:17.

How is God described in this verse?

What does it say about God's gifts?

One part of the relationship with our Heavenly Father that we often distort into something unhealthy is a misplaced affection for the things He gives us. We turn good things into gods and worship them, allowing them to consume our lives. Earlier, James warned that temptation and sin don't come from God, but from within our own hearts when we desire things instead of Him. It's true that gifts are from God (see Jas. 1:13-16). But the Giver is much greater than His gifts.

What are you tempted to put before God in your life?

You can recognize what you idolize by identifying what tempts you. If something is enticing, part of you believes it's more satisfying and pleasing than what God can give you. Whatever lures your heart away from loving your Heavenly Father is an idol and a distortion of His gifts.

Read Ephesians 1:3.

> **Why is it significant to know that believers have been blessed in Christ "with every spiritual blessing in the heavenly places"?**

Jesus is infinitely greater than anything in this world. He wants you to experience life to its fullest. And the things you think you want apart from Him aren't good. Jesus said:

> The thief comes only to steal and kill and destroy. I came that they may have life and have it abundantly. JOHN 10:10

Read Matthew 7:7-11.

No matter what your experiences are with fathers in this world, Jesus said you can trust your Heavenly Father. He knows what you need and wants to bless you with good gifts.

> **What are you worried about, fearing that God won't give you what you need? Do you worry that God will give you bad things?**

GOD'S GIFTS ARE GOOD. ENJOY THEM. BUT THE GIVER IS EVEN BETTER. ENJOY HIM MORE.

reflect

Take time to identify as many good things in your life as possible. Let your gratitude move beyond those good gifts to the even greater God who gave them to you.

💬 Share your thoughts: #JesusIsGreater

MORE THAN THIS WORLD
read

If God is a good Father who gives good gifts, why is life so bad at times? You don't have to watch the news or scroll through social media long to see what a mess the world is in.

What examples of brokenness do you see in this world?

A major problem with the Santa Claus image of God is that you have to assume when life is hard that you somehow deserve bad things. Or you conclude that God is either cruel with His power or powerless to do anything to help you. Scripture tells us that God is a good, loving, and all-powerful Father. This world is broken because of sin. But God is at work through Jesus to restore it all.

Read Revelation 21:1-5.

What hope exists in these verses?

Until that time, what do you do when life hurts? When you want to scream, cry, or shout to God, "Why?" Do it. Be honest. Let your cries drive you closer to God. What we really want in those moments is for God to fix it. What we really need is to know He's still with us and in control. Before we start to feel that God is a distant, impersonal Deity who can't understand or doesn't care that life is hard, remember that He came in the person of Jesus, lived among us, and died a cruel death on a cross for us. Jesus knows what we're going through. He's lived, suffered, and died. Then He rose again. He's alive with all power and authority in heaven and on earth. Our hope is in God's love for us in Jesus and the promise that all things will be made right:

> I have said these things to you, that in me you may have peace.
> In the world you will have tribulation.
> But take heart; I have overcome the world. JOHN 16:33

If you got everything you wanted, but didn't have Jesus, would you be satisfied? Would you have peace? Explain.

Read Matthew 6:25-34.

Our human inclination is to worry. We worry about anything we feel powerless to change or control. We even worry about the possibility that we might not have what we need for tomorrow.

What do you worry most about?

What hope did Jesus offer in this passage?

JESUS IS ENOUGH. HE IS OUR HOPE.

reflect

Cry out to God. Express your broken heart and concerns to Him in the space provided. Praise Him that He will make all things new and until that time, trust that Jesus is enough.

Share your thoughts: #JesusIsGreater

session four
COVENANT >
CONTRACT

"Covenant love is a love that implies deep commitment and promise. It's not based on feelings or on the other person's actions but on the initiating person's good pleasure."

start

Session three focused on idolatry, God as Father, and hope.

What was most helpful, encouraging, or challenging from your personal reading and reflection this past week?

In this session, we'll take an even deeper look at our relationship with God through Christ.

What is the most meaningful promise anyone has ever kept to you?

What is the worst experience you've ever had with a broken promise?

Relationships are built on trust. We know that everyone is imperfect—we'll let others down and we'll be let down. But Jesus is always faithful. Keep the following question in mind as you watch this week's video:

WHAT DOES A RELATIONSHIP WITH JESUS LOOK LIKE?

watch

USE THIS SPACE TO FOLLOW ALONG AS YOU WATCH "COVENANT>CONTRACT."

REMEMBER THIS 🎧

> A covenant is about the promise, not the behavior.
> A contract is about the behavior, not a promise.
> To be a Christian is about identity, not activity. Activity flows from that identity.
> Coming to Jesus is the beginning of the road, not the end.
> You are a child of the living God, under covenant, not contract.

THINK ABOUT THIS ❓

> Do you believe that God celebrates when you come home?
> Do you understand that you are a child of the living God who is under covenant, not contract?

LOOK IT UP 📖

> Luke 15:1-2, 11-32
> Matthew 23:23
> Romans 1:25
> Deuteronomy 7:9
> Genesis 3:8-9

consider

Do you believe you are accepted and loved unconditionally by God as His child? Or do you live with the fear that one day He may give up on you?

When have you felt you were one sin away from God giving up on you?

Read Luke 15:1-2.

Religion makes enemies. Jesus makes friends. Throughout His earthly ministry, Jesus reached out to those who were rejected or marginalized.

What encouragement or conviction does it give you to know that Jesus reached out to sinners and that they were drawn to Him?

Read Luke 15:11-32.

Are you more like the rebellious or entitled son in this story? In what ways?

When have you experienced the grace of the Heavenly Father?

How does understanding that you're a child under covenant, not under contract, change your view of God?

How does it change your view of sin and forgiveness to know that your Father celebrates your return?

Jeff explained that the gospel isn't just for saving you. The gospel is relevant every day, especially when you mess up.

List some ways you need Jesus each day.

Read Genesis 3:8-9.

What was man's response to sin? God's response?

respond

Starting right now, how can you come out of hiding, take off your mask, and experience the joy and freedom of Christ?

COVENANT > CONTRACT

Grace is scandalous. The fact that God loves the ungodly is unthinkable. But the fact that Jesus was a friend of sinners and was rejected by the religious is undeniable. Throughout scriptural history as well as today, people can't free themselves from sin. Salvation comes only by the grace of God through the blood of His Son, Jesus. No amount of moral conduct or religious ritual will ever earn abundant life in this world or eternity with God. We can be free from the slavery of our own efforts.

Truly grasping the freeing power of God's grace helps us realize the following truths:

1 Freedom is better than faking it.
2 Family is more than just a name.
3 Failure doesn't equal firing.

In Christ, there's no condemnation, no shame, no hiding, no mask. We're free to truly experience the love and grace of God and His people.

FOR MORE, READ CHAPTER 8 IN THE BOOK: *JESUS > RELIGION*.

FREEDOM IS BETTER THAN FAKING IT
read

Freedom. We're not talking red, white, and blue democracy. Being a Christian isn't about being a Republican, a Democrat, or even an American. While we can be grateful for political liberties in our country, an even greater freedom exists no matter where we live.

Freedom isn't the license to do whatever you want. That's slavery to your own self-centered desires—also known as sin. Jesus set you free from the ruthless master of your desires. That life wasn't working out too well. Turns out sin is a cruel master that always pays with death (see Rom. 6:15-23).

Freedom also isn't about flaunting or abusing your liberty as a Christian. Ironically, that is slavery to your so-called freedom.

Read Galatians 5:13-14.

When have you twisted freedom into a license to do whatever you wanted?

Jesus didn't pay the price for our sin just to have us become slaves to self-effort. Scripture is clear—and so are our personal experiences—that our natural tendency is toward religion. Toward effort. Control. Slavery. That's the very definition of insanity: doing the same thing and expecting different results. Our efforts couldn't save us. We could never earn God's approval through religion. We were set free from effort, illusions of control, and the slavery of religion, but we keep going back to the idea that we have to try harder and be good enough. Even if we believe we were saved by grace alone through faith, not works, we somehow buy into the lie that our relationship with Jesus is now up to us. Paul put it this way:

> Are you so foolish? Having begun by the Spirit, are you now being perfected by the flesh?
> GALATIANS 3:3

In what specific areas do you slip back into believing your relationship with God relies entirely on what you do?

Freedom is embracing truth, not keeping it at a distance. God justifies the ungodly (see Rom. 5:6). You don't have to pretend to be perfect. You need Jesus. You need His grace today just as much as you did when you first trusted Him to give you a new life. Stop faking it. Take off your mask. Run to Him.

Read Genesis 3:1-13.

It's natural to hide and pass the blame. The very first people on earth hid and then tried to pass the blame for the first sin ever committed against God. But in His love and grace, God knows us, comes to us, calls us out of hiding, and sets us free.

What are you still trying to hide? What in your life, if found out, would make you feel completely vulnerable and exposed?

It's just as pointless for you to think you can hide anything from God as it was for Adam and Eve to literally hide from Him behind a tree. God, the One who made you and knows everything about you, is inviting you out of the darkness and into the light.

NO MORE HIDING. NO MORE BLAMING. GOD IS CALLING YOU TO A BETTER LIFE. BE FREE.

reflect

What if you got honest about your need for grace? What freedom would exist if you didn't feel the pressure to prove yourself to God or others? Reflect on what you can do to start living in the freedom of Christ.

💬 Share your thoughts: #JesusIsGreater

FAMILY IS MORE THAN JUST A NAME
read

The Bible is clear that by God's gracious love, you aren't just called a child of God. You are His child. He's your Father. This is more than just nice, religious language. This is fact. This is family:

> See what kind of love the Father has given to us, that we should be called children of God; and so we are. 1 JOHN 3:1

This isn't religious effort. This is a brand-new identity. You don't try to be part of a family. You did nothing to deserve it or earn it. There are only two ways a child can be part of a family: birth and adoption. The Bible includes both ideas when describing your relationship with the Heavenly Father.

Read 1 John 5:1.

What does this verse say about being born into God's family?

Read John 1:12-13.

What do these verses say about being born into God's family?

Read Ephesians 1:5.

What does this verse say about your adoption into God's family?

Read Romans 8:15.

What does this verse say about your adoption into God's family?

A personal relationship with God isn't determined by what family you were born into physically, but by the deliberate act of your Heavenly Father's will for you to be born again spiritually. That's a point Jesus made in His conversation with Nicodemus, the religious leader born into the right Jewish family (see John 3:1-21). Scripture makes it clear that being born into God's family is completely tied to our belief in Jesus, God's Son. This is a result of the Father's will, not our own.

Adoption is also an act of the Father's will. He chooses you. Don't miss that. There are no accidents in the family of God. Human parents may not plan on the birth of a child and may not know what to do, but your Heavenly Father has a plan for every person He created. He knew exactly who you would be, when and where and to whom you would be born, and how He would adopt you into His family.

It's not about us—who we are or where we were born. It's about a loving Father who pursues us. Chooses us. Loves us. Unconditionally. Children adopted into a family have every right possessed by the children born into the family. They enjoy every provision, protection, blessing, and inheritance of the Father. No matter who the child was before, now they bear the Father's name.

How does knowing that God chose you and has a plan for your life give you hope for a future, regardless of your past or present?

God extends His love and family to include whoever believes in His Son. Being a Christian is more than just a name. It's a new identity. It's a relationship. It's an eternal inheritance.

THE BLOOD JESUS SHED IS GREATER THAN THE BLOOD IN YOUR VEINS. YOU'VE BEEN MADE PART OF HIS FAMILY. FOREVER.

reflect

Reflect on the fact that you're a child of God—by the grace of His will. Praise Him. Thank Him. Express your love to your Heavenly Father. Consider how living in relationship with a loving Heavenly Father and following His Son are different from just calling yourself a Christian.

Share your thoughts: #JesusIsGreater

FAILURE DOESN'T EQUAL FIRING
read

Jesus told His followers they weren't His servants—they weren't employees doing an assigned task—but they were His friends (see John 15:15). He chose them so that they could experience the Father's love. Jesus brought a group of normal people the world would have never chosen, with all their failures and flaws, into an intimate relationship. He knew them and they knew Him.

The same is true for you today. Jesus knows you. You can know Him. You have a personal relationship. You're not a servant blindly following instructions. You're part of something bigger and better than that. You can experience the life-changing love of the Father and share it with the world.

What feelings or attitudes result when you view your relationship with Jesus as similar to an employer and employee?

What do you currently view in your Christian life as a task, duty, or job assignment?

It's true that Jesus said our actions are an important part of our relationship with the Father. Scripture teaches obedience to the Father is an act of love and trust, revealing our identity as His children (see 1 John 5:3). But it isn't the begrudging duty of a reluctant employee. It's an act of faith in the One who proves Himself always faithful and infinitely greater than anything in this world.

One of the most famous biblical stories about the unconditional love of a father for his child is found in the Gospel of Luke. Jesus told a parable illustrating just how great the bond of family is and how we all seem to misunderstand the nature of a relationship with our Heavenly Father.

Read Luke 15:11-32.

In what ways have you acted ungratefully toward your Heavenly Father?

Are you more like the rebellious child or the proud, entitled child? Explain.

Both sons failed to appreciate their relationship with their father. But their failure didn't change the fact that they were family. They were in covenant—which is based on promise, not performance. Their father was greater than their failure. The covenant was greater than a contract.

The father disregarded the repentant son's request to be made a servant. The son wasn't demoted or fired, because he wasn't an employee. Neither can you be fired because of your failure. You're a child of the Father, of the King. And His love for you is extravagant and unconditional. Your identity as a child of the Father doesn't change. The good news of the gospel doesn't change either—it is more than good news that redeems you once; it continues to be good news that restores you each day:

> If we say we have no sin, we deceive ourselves, and the truth is not in us. If we confess our sins, he is faithful and just to forgive us our sins and to cleanse us from all unrighteousness. 1 JOHN 1:8-9

Confession brings freedom and restoration. The Father celebrates and blesses the child who turns from selfish attitudes to receive the joy of being in a right relationship with Him. You can't clean yourself up. But when you humble yourself, you realize He has open arms that are ready to embrace you. Repent, turn around, return to the Father, and enjoy celebrating life with Him.

THE FATHER'S FAITHFULNESS IS GREATER THAN YOUR FAILURES.

reflect

Psalm 13:5-6 describes God's love as unfailing, faithful, or steadfast. As you read these verses, allow yourself to feel overwhelmed by the Father's love. Express your thankfulness to God.

💬 Share your thoughts: #JesusIsGreater

WORSHIP >
RITUALS

"when we realize the beauty of God's grace in the mundane,
not just the religious, that's when we will begin to see
Him correctly."

start

Session four focused on freedom, family, and failure.

What was most helpful, encouraging, or challenging from your personal reading and reflection in session four?

Today, we'll begin looking at the practice of worship.

What do you think of when you hear the word *worship*?

There are certain elements or rituals that may be included in worship, but worship is more than just something done at a certain time or place. Keep the following question in mind as we watch the next video:

IF JESUS > RELIGION, WHAT DOES IT MEAN TO WORSHIP HIM?

watch

USE THIS SPACE TO FOLLOW ALONG AS YOU WATCH "WORSHIP > RITUALS."

REMEMBER THIS

> Good things can be distorted when we worship them.
> We are to worship God in spirit and in truth.
> God is breaking down the wall between the secular and sacred.
> It's not about sacred space, but about people who worship God correctly.
> In Jesus, we become the true temple.
> All of life is worship.

THINK ABOUT THIS

> Are you worshiping God correctly—in spirit and truth?
> Are you worshiping God in all of life?

LOOK IT UP

> 2 Corinthians 5:18-19
> Genesis 1, 2:15
> Exodus 20:3-5
> John 4:20-24
> 1 Corinthians 6:19, 10:31, 12:4
> 2 Corinthians 6:16
> 1 Timothy 4:4
> Matthew 7:11, 28:19
> Revelation 21:10

consider

Where else, besides Jesus, do people seek meaning and purpose in life?

What have you lived for in the past?

When have you wondered or even worried about God's will?

How do our previous discussions about freedom and God as a loving Father help you understand that His will is more like the boundaries of a circle than a precise point we have to get right?

We can overcomplicate God's will and what's right, holy, or considered ministry. God's will is specific about our general purpose but allows freedom in the practical, everyday details.

Read 2 Corinthians 5:18-19.

What do these verses identify as God's general will for our lives?

Read 1 Corinthians 6:19-20 and 2 Corinthians 6:16.

How does being the temple influence the way you see your life?

What does it mean not to be your own?

How does being the temple shape your understanding of worship?

Read 1 Corinthians 10:31.

What do you enjoy doing?

How can you worship God in that pursuit?

respond

How can you use your gifts, talents, and passions for God's glory?

WORSHIP> RITUALS

What does God want from us? How do we know His will? What is life all about? What gives our lives meaning? We often overcomplicate the answers to these questions. If everything God created is good, then we don't need to separate secular from sacred. To be a good Christian, you don't have to buy only Christian things, go to Christian schools, or get Christian jobs (while all those things may be good, they aren't required). You are uniquely created in the image of God. Do whatever you do, wherever you are, for the glory of God instead of for your own glory. Everything can be an act of worship, not just certain activities during a scheduled time at a certain location. Worship is more than a religious service. Worship is the way you live. Live intentionally and creatively to honor Christ.

Three things can help us wrap our hearts and minds around the fact that all of life is worship:

1 Your calling is more than a career.
2 God's will is more like a circle than a dot.
3 The One we worship is greater than where we worship.

FOR MORE, READ CHAPTER 9 IN THE BOOK: *JESUS > RELIGION*.

CALLING IS MORE THAN A CAREER
read

Ever see or hear the word *vocation*? That's a word we use today to describe a profession, right? Engineers. Lawyers. Doctors. Mechanics. Plumbers. Ministers.

Vocation means calling. It even looks like the word voice. Before it grew to include a broad spectrum of careers, the roots of the word were in the Christian community. People felt a calling from God to devote their lives to full-time service of the church.

But even before that, vocation originally referred to God's calling people to salvation—bringing the dead to life. It was responding to God's invitation to join His family. The voice of our Father calling His children into new life through a relationship with Jesus.

Read 1 Peter 2:9-10.

> **Do you feel a specific calling on your life? Are you drawn toward a specific career, cause, or area of interest? Explain.**

> **How could you share the light of Christ with others in daily life or through your specific interests?**

A lot of people take the idea of being holy, which means set apart for God, and take it to an extreme. They think being a good Christian means distancing themselves as far as possible from secular things and forming a weird little subculture—a Christian bubble.

Read John 17:15-21.

How can you be in the world, but not of it—set apart for God's purposes yet close to the people who need Jesus?

Often people think that to be a good Christian means you have to buy only Christian things, go to Christian schools, study Christian subjects, and even get Christian jobs. Maybe you've even wondered whether God was calling you into ministry. And yes, some people are definitely called into professional areas of service like preachers or missionaries (see Eph. 4:11). But really, every Christian is in ministry. Our ministries just look different. Some are called to be Christian bakers, entrepreneurs, artists, educators, or stay-at-home parents. But no matter what specialty you're in, it's less about the work you do and more about who you represent as you do it.

Read 2 Corinthians 5:13-21.

If you've ever worried that you might look crazy doing what you love and following Jesus 100 percent, be encouraged. Paul wrote that it's OK to be misunderstood. Everybody isn't going to get your decision to follow Jesus. But everyone should be able to see Jesus in you.

How can you represent Jesus within your circle of influence?

YOUR CALLING IS TO KNOW JESUS AND TO MAKE HIM KNOWN.

reflect

Consider how God has wired you—your personality, experiences, talents, and interests. Thank God for the way He created you. Ask Him to reveal how He wants to use your unique qualities in His kingdom work.

💬 Share your thoughts: #JesusIsGreater

MORE LIKE A CIRCLE THAN A DOT
read

Do you have freedom to do what you want? Or does God have a plan for your life? Yes. And yes.

God's will often feels elusive and confusing. We may not think about God's will at all because we don't believe in God, don't believe He has a plan for our lives, or don't believe we can figure it out.

Or on the opposite end of the spectrum, we obsess over God's will—even to the point of being paralyzed with fear—scared to step out of bounds. We fear that if we make the wrong choice, God will punish us for being out of His will. Life then becomes like walking through a field of land mines, each step an act of faith that you desperately hope doesn't blow up in your face.

On a scale of 0 to 10, how often do you think about God's will for your life?

0   1   2   3   4   5   6   7   8   9   10

never   **obsessively**

Read Romans 12:2.

What does this verse say about knowing God's will?

Read Romans 8:26-29.

How do these verses help you understand God's will?

Not only is it possible to know God's will, but He desires for us to know His will. In fact, He helps us know His will through the work of the Holy Spirit. God's good, pleasing, and perfect will for your life is to be conformed to the image of His Son, Jesus.

Read John 6:29 and 1 Thessalonians 5:18.

How do these verses describe God's will for us as believers?

Too often we overcomplicate God's will for our lives. We think of God's will as a dot requiring pinpoint accuracy. But thinking of His will more like a circle better fits how Scripture describes it.

Read Psalm 37:3-4.

You're a unique child of God. He wants you to grow and express yourself within the healthy boundaries He has provided. Doing God's will is a natural part of being in God's family. When your desires become the same as God's desires, He gladly gives you what you want and need—more of Him. When you want Him more than anything else, everything you do within the circle God has drawn becomes an act of worship. Paul put it this way:

> Whatever you do, in word or deed, do everything in the name of the Lord Jesus,
> giving thanks to God the Father through him. COLOSSIANS 3:17

GOD WANTS MORE FOR YOU—MORE JOY, FREEDOM, LIFE. HE WANTS TO MAKE YOU MORE LIKE JESUS.

reflect

Draw a circle and write the words "God's will" inside. Talk to God about the decisions (big and small) you are facing right now. Ask for wisdom to glorify Him in every situation.

💬 Share your thoughts: #JesusIsGreater

THE ONE WE WORSHIP IS GREATER THAN WHERE WE WORSHIP
read

Worship is more than gathering at a designated time and place and using a certain style of music. It's not about when, where, or how we worship; it's about whom we worship. It's about the posture of our hearts. It's about lifting up the name of Jesus as our ultimate desire.

You may have a worship style that's most natural for expressing yourself. It's good to be fully engaged in worship and surrounded by a community of brothers and sisters in Christ. Just remember that it's not a show. It's not about impressing people; it's about glorifying Him.

What helps you focus your heart and mind on Jesus in worship?

It's easy to forget that worship is all about Jesus. Worship isn't about our preferences or convenience. To learn more, let's revisit the passage about Jesus' encounter with the woman at the well.

Read John 4:19-26.

Worship is defined by glory and thanksgiving. We're worshiping when we give glory or ultimate value to something. This can be a job, a relationship, sports, anything. And whatever we give glory to, we're willing to sacrifice for.

As true worshipers, worshiping in spirit and in truth, we become the temple. Paul made this clear in his letter to the Christians in Corinth:

> Do you not know that you are God's temple and that God's Spirit dwells in you?
> 1 CORINTHIANS 3:16

Read 1 Corinthians 6:19-20.

How does seeing yourself as God's temple shape your view of worship?

Does your lifestyle represent the fact that your body is God's temple? Explain.

The presence of your Savior is with you right now. Let that sink in. Jesus, Emmanuel, God with us—He's with you. Literally. Powerfully. And He alone is worthy of all praise, honor, and glory.

Read Revelation 21:1-7.

Jesus is the Alpha and Omega. That's the Greek alphabet's equivalent of saying He's the A through Z. He's the first, last, and everything in between. For Jesus to desire your worship isn't egotistical or vain. It's actually an act of love. He desires what's best for you. To give our ultimate devotion and affection to anything other than Jesus always steals, kills, and destroys the abundance found only in a relationship with Him (see John 10:10). It's in your best interest to worship Him. He can completely satisfy you in ways nothing in this world can.

Everything you do is an act of worship, giving glory to Jesus or to something infinitely less worthy—which is idolatry and sin. Your body is the holy place where the presence and power of a holy God dwells on earth.

YOUR LIFE IS YOUR WORSHIP OF JESUS. BE HOLY BECAUSE HE IS HOLY.

reflect

Spend a few minutes (or more) filling your heart and mind with the greatness of God and the amazing reality that His Spirit lives in you.

Share your thoughts: #JesusIsGreater

session six
COMMUNITY >
CONFORMITY

"The church is a place to be transparent and vulnerable. The church is a place to take off the mask. The church is a place you can be yourself."

start

Session five focused on your calling, God's will, and worship.

What was most helpful, encouraging, or challenging from your personal reading and reflection in session five?

We'll begin with a look at life in community—which comes from the word "common."

What do you share in common with the students in this group? What are some differences?

In Jesus, what we have in common is greater than our differences. That is at the heart of community. The unity and diversity of the church should be a beautiful thing. Unfortunately, church is one of the most misunderstood parts of a relationship with Jesus, today.

Each session is intended to help you set aside preconceived ideas and experiences with things we may associate with religion—Jesus, the Bible, worship, holiness, etc. As we start wrapping up our study of *Jesus > Religion*, keep in mind the following question as you watch this final video:

IF JESUS > RELIGION, WHY IS THE CHURCH SO IMPORTANT?

watch

USE THIS SPACE TO FOLLOW ALONG AS YOU WATCH "COMMUNITY > CONFORMITY."

REMEMBER THIS 💬

> You were created for community.
> Trying to live without community is like trying to live without oxygen.
> The church is God's agent to reconcile the world to Himself.
> The church is the body of Christ. Jesus is the head of the body.
> A body works best if everything is doing separate things pointing toward the greater cause.

THINK ABOUT THIS ❓

> What if, instead of thinking we exist for our own benefit, we saw the church as existing for what it really is—the bride and body of Christ, showing His love and grace to all who need it.

LOOK IT UP 📖

> Genesis 1:26
> 2 Corinthians 5:19-20
> Matthew 16:18
> Acts 2:37-47
> Galatians 3:28, 6:2
> 1 Corinthians 12:4-6, 12-20, 25-26
> Ephesians 2:13, 4:15, 5:25-27
> Romans 12:10
> Hebrews 10:24-25
> Revelation 19:7

consider

Jeff opened the video saying that by God's design we're created for community.

Which illustration do you best relate to? Why?

○ Life without community is like life without oxygen.
○ Life without community is like sitting on a one-legged stool.
○ Life in community is like a family.

The diversity of the early church was a scandalous community like the world had never seen.

Read 1 Corinthians 12:4-6, 12-20, 25-26, and Galatians 3:28.

What encouragement does Paul's description of diversity and unity give you as part of Jesus' body—His church?

Read Matthew 16:13-18.

Various opinions have always existed about Jesus' identity. Confessing the truth of Jesus as the Christ, the Son of God, is the common ground on which the church is built.

How would you explain to someone who Jesus is? How has this study helped you know and love Jesus more?

How would you explain what Jesus meant when He said the gates of hell wouldn't prevail against His church?

Read Romans 12:10, Galatians 6:2, and Hebrews 10:24-25.

What actions are explicitly taught in each of these verses as characteristic of true Christian community?

When and how have you experienced this kind of community?

respond

How can this group be that kind of community to one another?

COMMUNITY> CONFORMITY

Life shouldn't be lived alone. It's better together. We've seen that religious activities in and of themselves have no value, but when Christ is the focus of our lives and the desire of our hearts, believers will be drawn together as a community to celebrate Him and to experience more of Him.

If the church is the body and bride of Christ, then we can't love the Head without the body. A healthy church isn't a club for clones, forcing conformity. It's a vibrant and diverse community brought together by Jesus. And having Jesus in common is greater than any differences that exist among us. Individual members of the body are encouraged to love the community of Christ, joining other followers of Jesus so that the many parts can work together to grow to maturity and provide shelter for those who are hurting and in need.

Jesus' plan to share His love with the world is the church. The church isn't an institutional subculture that withdraws from the world, but a light that engages the culture, offering the love and joy of Christ.

1 Life is better together.
2 The body is more than any one part.
3 The light of Jesus is greater than darkness.

FOR MORE, READ CHAPTER 10 IN THE BOOK: *JESUS > RELIGION.*

LIFE IS BETTER TOGETHER
read

The narrative of Scripture begins with a beautiful rhythm in creation. God, the holy Trinity—Father, Son, and Holy Spirit—made everything from nothing. Light. Good. Sky and sea. Good. Land and everything that grows on it. Good. Orderly solar system. Good. Creatures swimming in the water and flying in the air. Good. Creatures living on dry land. Good.

Everything was good. The Hebrew language has a word for the peace and balance that characterized God's original creation: *shalom*. Harmony. Rhythm. Order. Everything was created in its place by design and with purpose. Seven times God pronounced His creation "good," with the last description being "very good." This "very good" came after the following:

> God said, "Let us make man in our image, after our likeness. And let them have dominion over the fish of the sea and over the birds of the heavens and over the livestock and over all the earth and over every creeping thing that creeps on the earth." So God created man in his own image, in the image of God he created him; male and female he created them. GENESIS 1:26-27

Look at the Scripture again. Circle every plural pronoun.

Why is it significant that God and people are relational beings?

The first time anything in Scripture is described as not good, even before sin entered the world, was when Adam was alone in the work God had given him. He needed community.

Read Genesis 2:18.

Man and woman were designed as perfect counterparts, created in the glorious image of God and complementing each other in their work together. They enjoyed life together and were unashamed, one flesh, with nothing to hide.

But the honeymoon was over in the next chapter. Together, Adam and Eve gave in to temptation. As a result, they went into hiding. They felt shame. Relationships were broken. Work became challenging. Life became difficult (see Gen. 3). But God called them out of hiding. And check this out: the original Greek word for church in the New Testament—*ekklesia*—literally means *people called out.*

The church is a community of people called out of sin and shame; called out of death and darkness and given new life. The good order of creation is being restored in the community of those called out by God. Together we can resist sin and do the work of God as His image-bearers in the world.

Life without community is like trying to sit on a stool with only one leg. It's exhausting and misses the point of the design. You were made for relationships with God and His people. Jesus didn't leave us as orphans without a home and without hope (see John 14:1-18). Our hope is in the gospel. That's what we share as the common bond of Christian community. We aren't left to figure out good and evil, right and wrong, life and death on our own.

Read Hebrews 10:23-25 and Romans 12:9-21.

How is community described in these passages?

WHY SETTLE FOR ANYTHING LESS THAN LIFE TOGETHER IN COMMUNITY?

reflect

What can you do to build community and show appreciation for the people in your life? Get creative.

Share your thoughts: #JesusIsGreater

THE BODY IS MORE THAN ONE PART
read

The apostle Paul used a particular image in his letters to help Christians understand their role as a community of faith. The picture is both humorous and beautiful, convicting yet encouraging.

Read 1 Corinthians 12:12-20.

What did Paul write in verses 12-13 about being a Christian?

What encouragement does this image of the body give you, especially if you've ever felt like you didn't fit in at church?

When we think of church, we often think of a building when we should think of a body. Religion turns it into a club when it's really about Christ. The church isn't about conformity, but community.

Read 1 Corinthians 12:21-27.

Sometimes it's easy to think that we have to be exactly like everyone else. We can slip back into the cycle of comparison and frustration, feeling we're not good enough to serve God. Or on the other end of the spectrum, we can become proud and conceited, thinking that people who aren't exactly like us, are not really Christians—or at least not very good ones. But Paul is clear that both views are not only unnatural, but also absurd. Not only do you fit in the church, but the church also needs you. Whatever part you play, the body works together and needs every member to be fully alive, healthy, and functional.

Read Romans 12:3-5.

Which extreme do you lean toward—feeling that you don't fit in and aren't important to the church or feeling that others aren't as important as you?

No matter who you are, what you've done, what you've suffered, or when you started following Jesus, you're valued. You're part of His body. You're fearfully and wonderfully made for a reason. God has a plan and a purpose for you.

The goal of the church is a healthy, mature, growing body. Not only does the church need you, but you also need the church. It's a mutually beneficial relationship.

> Put on then, as God's chosen ones, holy and beloved, compassionate hearts, kindness, humility, meekness, and patience, bearing with one another and, if one has a complaint against another, forgiving each other; as the Lord has forgiven you, so you also must forgive. And above all these put on love, which binds everything together in perfect harmony. And let the peace of Christ rule in your hearts, to which indeed you were called in one body. And be thankful. Let the word of Christ dwell in you richly, teaching and admonishing one another in all wisdom, singing psalms and hymns and spiritual songs, with thankfulness in your hearts to God.
> COLOSSIANS 3:12-16

In the previous verses, circle every word that describes the attitudes and actions that should characterize the body of Christ.

YOU'RE PART OF SOMETHING BIGGER THAN YOURSELF. YOU MATTER.

reflect

You can't be a Christian and hate the church or say you don't need it. You're part of the body. So it should be natural to take care of it and make sure it's healthy. (See Eph. 5:29-30.) Reflect on what it means to be a part of the body of Jesus in this world.

💬 Share your thoughts: #JesusIsGreater

LIGHT IS GREATER THAN DARKNESS
read

> The light shines in the darkness, and the darkness has not overcome it ... The true light, which gives light to everyone, was coming into the world. He was in the world, and the world was made through him, yet the world did not know him. He came to his own, and his own people did not receive him. But to all who did receive him, who believed in his name, he gave the right to become children of God, who were born, not of blood nor of the will of the flesh nor of the will of man, but of God. And the Word became flesh and dwelt among us, and we have seen his glory, glory as of the only Son from the Father, full of grace and truth.
> JOHN 1:5,9-14

This is the gospel. Jesus isn't just a good man, religious teacher, social activist, moral role model, or historical figure. He's the Son of the Father. He's God. He's the Creator of everything—including you. He has always existed. But He humbled Himself to become part of His own creation. He became a man. Fully human. Fully God. Light. Truth. Grace. In the flesh.

What darkness do you see in the world?

What hope is found in knowing darkness can't overcome the light of Jesus?

No matter how bad things may get, the darkness won't prevail. Even in history's darkest hour, when Jesus died, the darkness didn't win. Jesus was wrapped in grave clothes and laid in a tomb sealed by a gigantic stone. His dead body was guarded by Roman soldiers. But three days later, on Sunday morning, Jesus was alive. Resurrected. Glorious. The light pierced the darkness.

Think about it from a purely literal and scientific perspective. Darkness doesn't dim light. Light affects darkness. Chases it away. Darkness is simply an absence of light. It's impossible for darkness to overcome light.

If there are dark places in your life, let the Light in. Let Jesus transform every part of your life.

Read John 8:12.

What promise does Jesus make to His followers?

Read John 9:5 and Matthew 5:14-16.

What do these verses tell us about the light of Jesus?

Christianity isn't as individualistic as some people want you to believe. Yes, your faith is a personal relationship with Jesus, but it isn't private. Jesus is the light of the world. There's no hiding that fact once His Spirit empowers you to bring His light to the darkness.

If Jesus really is all the things we've seen over the past six weeks, then you have to make a decision. Regardless of what anyone else believes, you have to decide what you believe about Jesus.

Read Matthew 16:13-18.

Jesus is building His church on this confession of faith. He promises that the gates of hell won't prevail against the church. He promises that the darkness won't overcome you as His follower. You have a mission. The church is God's plan A. There is no plan B.

YOU ARE THE CHURCH. YOU'RE THE LIGHT OF THE WORLD. AND THE DARKNESS IS LOSING.

reflect

Who do you say Jesus is? What will you tell people about Jesus?

💬 Share your thoughts: #JesusIsGreater

CONCLUSION

As you wrap up this study, think about what you have learned or been challenged to consider over the last six weeks. Answer the following:

Is Jesus > Religion in your life? Explain.

How would you explain the difference between having religion and having a relationship with Jesus?

What are some key truths from this study that impacted your life?

How are you going to live differently because of what you have learned?

WHY I HATE RELIGION BUT LOVE JESUS
Poem by Jefferson Bethke

What if I told you Jesus came to abolish religion?
What if I told you voting Republican really wasn't His mission?
What if I told you Republican doesn't automatically mean Christian,
And just because you call some people blind doesn't automatically give you vision.
I mean, if religion is so great, why has it started so many wars?
Why does it build huge churches but fail to feed the poor?
Tells single moms God doesn't love them if they've ever had a divorce,
But in the Old Testament God actually calls religious people whores.

Religion might preach grace, but another thing they practice,
Tend to ridicule God's people; they did it to John the Baptist.
They can't fix their problems, and so they just mask it,
Not realizing religion is like spraying perfume on a casket.
See, the problem with religion is that it never gets to the core.
It's just behavior modification, like a long list of chores.
Like let's dress up the outside, make it look nice and neat,
But it's funny that's what they used to do to mummies while the corpse rots underneath.

Now I ain't judging; I'm just saying quit putting on a fake look,
Because there's a problem if people only know that you're a Christian by your Facebook.
I mean, in every other aspect of life, you know that logic's unworthy.
It's like saying you play for the Lakers just because you bought a jersey.
See, this was me too, but no one seemed to be on to me,
Acting like church kid while addicted to pornography.
See, on Sunday I'd go to church but Saturday getting faded,
As if I was simply created to have sex and get wasted.
See, I spent my whole life building this façade of neatness,
But now that I know Jesus, I boast in my weakness.

Because if grace is water, then the church should be an ocean.
It's not a museum for good people; it's a hospital for the broken.
Which means I don't have to hide my failures; I don't have to hide my sin,
Because it doesn't depend on me, it depends on Him.
See, when I was God's enemy and certainly not a fan,
He looked down and said, "I want that man!"

Which is why Jesus hated religion, and for it He called them fools.
Don't you see He's so much better than just following some rules?
Now let me clarify: I love the church, I love the Bible, and yes, I believe in sin,
But if Jesus came to your church, would they actually let Him in?
Remember, He was called a glutton and a drunkard by "religious men,"
But the Son of God never supports self-righteousness—not now, not then.

Now back to the point; one thing is vital to mention:
How Jesus and religion are on opposite spectrums.
One's the work of God, and one's a manmade invention.
One is the cure, but the other's the infection.
Because religion says do; Jesus says done.
Religion says slave; Jesus says son.
Religion puts you in bondage, but Jesus sets you free.
Religion makes you blind, but Jesus makes you see.

And that is why religion and Jesus are two different clans.
Religion is man searching for God, but Christianity is God searching for man.
Which is why salvation is freely mine, and forgiveness is my own,
Not based on my merits but Jesus' obedience alone.
Because He took the crown of thorns and the blood that dripped down His face.
He took what we all deserved; I guess that's why you call it grace.
While being murdered, He yelled, "Father, forgive them; they know not what they do."
Because when He was dangling on that cross, He was thinking of you.
He absorbed all your sin, and He buried it in the tomb.
Which is why I'm kneeling at the cross now saying, "Come on; there's room."

So for religion, know I hate it; in fact, I literally resent it.
Because when Jesus said, "It is finished," I believe He meant it.

> **Watch Jefferson recite this poem at www.youtube.com/bball1989**

**LAW-KEEPING
DUTY
OBLIGATION
PERFORMANCE
WORKS
RELIGION
ATTENDANCE
RULES**

There's so much more to Jesus than this. Perfect attendance, perfect performance—none of it works. Dead, dry rule keeping keeps us from embracing this simple promise: We are fully known and deeply loved. Join Bethke for a 6-week study as he unpacks the differences between teeth gritting and grace, law and love, performance and peace, despair and hope.

lifeway.com/jesusisgreater
800.458.2772 | LifeWay Christian Stores

JESUS > RELIGION
THE BIBLE STUDY
JEFFERSON BETHKE

ALSO FOR ADULTS!

LifeWay | Adult